WORKING
THEN AND NOW

by Robin Nelson

first step nonfiction

⌐ Lerner Publications Company · Minneapolis

People work to **earn** money.

Working has changed
over time.

Long ago, people walked to work.

Now, people ride to work.

Long ago, some workers
wore name tags.

Now, many workers wear
ID badges.

Long ago, workers used paper.

Now, many workers use **computers**.

Long ago, farmers used
animals in the fields.

Now, farmers use **tractors**
and other machines.

Long ago, most women
worked at home.

Now, women work
everywhere.

Long ago, many children
worked in **factories**.

Now, most children go to school.

Long ago, work could be very dangerous.

Now, work is safer.

Working Timeline

1938
It becomes illegal for children to work.

1882
First Labor Day honors workers.

1938
First minimum wage (the least you can pay someone) is 25¢ an hour.

1939–1945
World War II—
Many women
go to work
while men fight
in the war.

1963
It becomes illegal
to pay men and
women different
amounts for the
same job.

1955
Minimum
wage is
$1.00 an
hour.

Working Facts

 There are many places to work. You can work in an office, store, or school. You can work outdoors. You can work at home. You can travel all over the world to do your work.

 Some people work during the day, and some people work at night.

 Some people work without earning any money. They are called volunteers.

Jobs can provide services. Services help others. Teachers, firefighters, and doctors provide services.

 Jobs can produce goods. Goods are things that can be sold. Farmers, artists, and carpenters make goods.

 The first computer was so big that it took up a whole room! Today, computers are so small you can hold them in your hand.

Glossary

 computers – machines that store and work with information

 earn – get paid money for work you do

 factories – buildings where things are made

 ID badges – cards worn to show who people are

 tractors – vehicles with big wheels that help farmers do jobs

Index

The images in this book are used with the permission of: National Archives, front cover, pp. 14, 22 (middle); © James Leynse/CORBIS, pp. 2, 22 (second from top); © Schenectady Museum; Hall of Electrical History Foundation/CORBIS, p. 3; © Arthur Rothstein/CORBIS, p. 4; © Philip James Corwin/CORBIS, p. 5; © George Marks/Retrofile/Getty Images, p. 6; © Siri Stafford/Riser/Getty Images, pp. 7, 22 (second from bottom); © H. Armstrong Roberts/Retrofile/Getty Images, p. 8; © age fotostock/SuperStock, pp. 9, 22 (top); AP Photo, p. 10; Courtesy John Deere & Company, pp. 11, 22 (bottom); Library of Congress, p. 12 (LC-DIG-nclc-04218); © Robert E. Daemmrich/Stone/Getty Images, p. 13; © Brian Summers/First Light/Getty Images, p. 15; © Bettmann/CORBIS, p. 16; © Chris Selby/Alamy, p. 17.

Lerner Publications Company
A division of Lerner Publishing Group, Inc.
241 First Avenue North
Minneapolis, MN 55401 U.S.A.

Website address: www.lernerbooks.com

Library of Congress Cataloging-in-Publication Data

Nelson, Robin, 1971–
    Working then and now / by Robin Nelson.
        p.   cm. — (First step nonfiction : then and now)
    Includes index.
    ISBN-13: 978–0–8225–8604–3 (lib. bdg. : alk. paper)
    1. Work—Juvenile literature. 2. Occupations—Juvenile literature. I. Title.
HD4851.N445 2008
306.3'6—dc22   2007017101

Manufactured in the United States of America
1 2 3 4 5 6 – DP – 13 12 11 10 09 08